Little

C000082288

British Commonwealth Edition
Published by Scripture Union
London, England.

North American Edition Including Canada
Published by Regal Books
A Division of G/L Publications
Ventura, California, USA

© Gordon Stowell 1984

First Edition 1984. Reprinted 1987, 1988

Co-edition arranged with the help of
Angus Hudson, London

Printed and Bound in Great Britain by
Purnell Book Production Ltd., Paulton, Bristol

Little Fish Books about You and Me

Help me
God

illustrated by Gordon Stowell

Help me God

to be a helper.

Help me to share my toys

with my friends.

Help me to take turns.

Help me to be patient.

Help me to be kind

to everyone.

Help me to love others

even when it is hard.

Help me to be cheerful

when things go wrong.

Help me to learn

more about you.

Help me to love all creatures

in Your world.

Thank You God

for all Your help.

It's fun

Little Fish Books about You and Me

Please God

Little Fish Books about You and Me

God knows

Little Fish Books about You and Me

Thank You God

Little Fish Books about You and Me

 Little Fish Books